Dynamic Discipline

Leadership Planners Series

Future-Proof Your Team

Win 'Em Over

Dynamic Discipline

Leadership Planners

Dynamic Discipline

CATHERINE HAKALA-AUSPERK

ALA
Editions
CHICAGO | 2019

CATHERINE HAKALA-AUSPERK is an author and national library speaker and consultant. She teaches at Kent State University's iSchool, as well as for the American Library Association's Certified Public Library Administrator (CPLA) program and many other organizations. She is the author of *Renew Yourself! A Six-Step Plan for More Meaningful Work, Build a Great Team: One Year to Success, Be a Great Boss: One Year to Success*, and this leadership planner series. Her passions are for supporting, coaching, and developing great libraries, successful teams, and—especially—strong and effective library leaders. You can follow her on Facebook at https://www.facebook.com/librariesthrive or on her website, librariesthrive.com.

© 2019 by the American Library Association

Extensive effort has gone into ensuring the reliability of the information in this book; however, the publisher makes no warranty, express or implied, with respect to the material contained herein.

ISBN: 978-0-8389-1832-6 (paper)

Library of Congress Cataloging in Publication Control Number: 2019006277

Book design by Alejandra Diaz in the Expo Serif Pro and Fira Sans typefaces.

♾ This paper meets the requirements of ANSI/NISO Z39.48–1992 (Permanence of Paper).

Printed in the United States of America
23 22 21 20 19   5 4 3 2 1

ALA Editions purchases fund advocacy, awareness, and accreditation programs for library professionals worldwide.

For all leaders who believe people are worth the effort.
You're right.

Dynamic.
(of a process or system) characterized by constant change, activity,
or progress.

—OXFORD ENGLISH DICTIONARY

Contents

AUTHOR'S NOTE

There are more of these leadership planners in the works. You can help make each one better than the next! Please send your feedback, criticism, suggestions, and topic ideas to me. What kind of leadership success would you like to plan?

chakalaausperk@gmail.com

It wasn't raining
when Noah
built the ark.

—RICHARD CUSHING

Why Plan?

NO ONE PLANS TO FAIL BUT, ODDLY ENOUGH, FEW PEOPLE PLAN TO SUCCEED. Using the planners in this series, you can do just that.

Planners are making a comeback (if they ever really went away). Even though we have high-tech tools we can use to chart our lives, todays' planners are bright and engaging. Why use them? There are as many answers as there are lines on which to write.

Planners, experts tell us, can help us to get and stay organized, make more intentional choices, be more productive, waste less time, reduce stress, and provide the time and tools that can help us solve today's challenges.

These planners are designed for library leaders who are facing some pretty serious challenges but haven't even had the chance to close their doors, sit back, untangle their issues, and begin to think about how to make things better.

Write in this book. Think of it as a combination to-do list, diary, and surrogate hairdresser or bartender (or any other good listener) that can provide you with the space, advice, and the luxury of time to think things through.

By the time you've finished all the readings and exercises, you will not have solved your problems. But you will be ready to *start* solving them—*and* you'll have a plan to do so.

The beatings will continue
until morale improves.

—CAPTAIN BLIGH

Dynamic Discipline

AS SOON AS you settle into your new leadership position, you're likely to find several things waiting for you. Shiny new business cards? Maybe. An uncomfortable polo shirt complete with logo? Probably. Personnel problems that previous leaders have ignored and let simmer, fester, and grow? Almost certainly. Why is that?

First, it's human nature. We are social animals, and, as such, we tend to shy away from situations that are uncomfortable or even potentially threatening. Second, we also like to be liked. And no one enjoys being criticized, even if it's justified. Finally, it's a question of preparation.

We can be trained how to hire. We can be trained how to manage work. We can be trained to oversee budgets. But we are rarely trained to handle problems before they occur, especially those we've not seen before and probably couldn't have imagined in our wildest dreams. And yet, there are some realities that will require us to learn how to discipline.

- ✔ Healthy teams resolve problems.
- ✔ Negativity can spread like wet stuff in a book drop.
- ✔ Productivity suffers when respect, safety, and honesty go out the window.
- ✔ It's your job.

The good news is that *discipline* does not have to be a dirty word. We aren't putting professional adults in "time out" here. When we focus on improvement—not punishment—even the greenest leader can discipline well.

If you want to change things,
you can't please everyone.
If you do please everyone,
you aren't making
enough progress.

—MARK ZUCKERBERG

Plan to Understand Why We Don't Discipline

THERE ARE PLENTY of popular excuses thrown around to rationalize why it's okay to avoid solving personnel problems, especially if the solution might involve discipline. It's important to remember that these justifications are rarely concocted by dastardly fiends, but more often by well-meaning, well-intentioned leaders who just don't what else to do or say.

Let's take a closer look at some of the more popular rationalizations that discourage us from fixing a problem—even while we're watching it continuing to grow, fester, and even spread throughout the workplace culture. These don't stand out because they are obscure, unreasonable, or "out-there" excuses. Quite the contrary. They're simple, common, and real enough to stop even the most determined leaders from doing what they know needs to be done.

- ✔ Someone will be mad at me.
- ✔ No one will back me up.
- ✔ Improvement is impossible.
- ✔ It's too late.
- ✔ I have no idea how to fix this.

Even if these aren't real possibilities, they may be real fears. So, what are our options? As Zig Ziglar once said, the word *fear* can stand for one of two things: *forget everything and run* or *face everything and rise*. It's not hard to figure out which one a great leader should choose.

It might help to take a closer look at each option to determine how true it is:

- ✔ No one goes into management for the sole purpose of making friends. Rather than wanting to be liked, leaders should be more concerned about being fair, professional, and respected. Solving problems is a great first step towards those goals.
- ✔ You're not completely on your own. Never. If your supervisor can't support you after you've made your case thoroughly and professionally, then maybe discipline is something you shouldn't be doing—yet. Find out what she thinks should be the next step and go from there. Or if you're the top boss, reach out to a peer or colleague with more experience and simply ask, "Help!"

✔ Nothing is impossible. Once all other avenues are exhausted, even the most serious personnel issues can be solved by allowing a person to find success elsewhere (translation: *fire him*.) That is improvement, after all.

✔ Repeat "it's never too late." I believe that by focusing on the language you use, every day can be the day change begins. If you're new, you could say, "I want to clarify right away the type of culture I'll be developing." If you've been there for years, try, "I've made a decision to change the course of our team culture. Here's what will be acceptable going forward." Just keep trying!

✔ You'll know what to do when you finish this planner—or take advantage of any other opportunities you can find to grow and develop your skills. And don't forget that your most valuable learning tool might be a colleague across town or someone you met at the last conference you attended. Reach out, find support, build skills, and improve the situation.

YOUR LINE IN THE SAND

A librarian was complaining one day about a certain teenager who caused trouble in the library every single day. Her three-warning limit had been exhausted months ago, and yet she returned every day, got three more warnings, and was then asked to leave. Again. Why, someone asked, was she allowed to continually break rules that she clearly knew? Good question.

In another group discussion, a manager bemoaned her difficulties with a certain team member who provided excellent service when at the desk but was habitually late to work. She couldn't possibly discipline him, could she? After all, he did his work well. The entire situation begs the question: did the team member know the consequence for lateness? Because he'd never experienced any consequence, the answer was no.

No conversation about using discipline to enforce performance expectations would be complete (nor even begin) without clarifying exactly what the rules are. Where is the performance line in the sand? Sometimes we generically address this, but we are rarely crystal clear.

So, start there. You're going to want to make sure that performance expectations and rules of discipline are simple, clear, and transparent. New employees must be required to first read, and then sign, a document stating that they understand these expectations and the consequences of not fulfilling them. Existing staff should be required to review them annually. And by all means, *keep it simple!* In one library, for example, the list of customer conduct infractions that would result in eviction ran a full three pages. It included restrictions on spitting, eating, running, jumping, and everything else up to and practically including standing on their heads. It was clarified, simplified, and rewritten to state that: (1) no one may cause a disruption in the library; (2) staff will determine what constitutes a disruption; and (3) disruptive patrons will be asked to leave. Period. Simple. Clear. With these rules, everyone would know where they stood.

The Worst That Could Happen

Sometimes even well-meaning bosses don't handle a problem or discipline well right off the bat. They might even think their initial knee-jerk reactions don't matter. But they do. Consider, and then enter, the worst possible impacts that might result from each of the six reactions listed. How might these responses, which are, by the way, the opposite of Improvement Discipline (ID), impact a team?

OPTIONS	RESULTS
Pretend You Don't Know	_____ _____ _____
Leave It for the Next Person to Solve	_____ _____ _____
Just Solve Half of the Problem . . . the Easy Half	_____ _____ _____
Yell and Scream	_____ _____ _____
Blame Others	_____ _____ _____
Re-Assign the Person to Another Place	_____ _____ _____

Keep It Simple

To be understood, we need to be clear. Don't allow confusion to be one of the reasons you don't discipline. Clearly communicate all elements of the discipline process both orally and in writing. Spell out expectations and consequences plainly. The first statement shows how language can become too complicated. In the opposite balloon, rewrite each statement using simplified, easy-to-understand language.

Some performance, conduct, or safety incidents are so problematic and harmful that the most effective action may be to remove the customer or employee (albeit temporarily) from the facility.

You may be sent home.

Where alleged misconduct has been investigated under another policy (e.g., dignity and respect, fraud and misappropriation, research misconduct, theft, bullying), the initial fact-finding and formal investigations carried out under that policy will constitute the investigation stages referred to in this policy.

Corrective action is a process designed to identify and correct problems that affect an employee's work performance or overall performance within the department or larger organization.

The employee will be given written documentation, signed by both the immediate supervisor and her immediate supervisor, regarding the suspension in relation to the undesirable behavior or action if it has been discussed in a previous verbal or written warning or the behavior or action was very severe in nature.

It should be explained to the employee that the incident will not go into his official personnel file, but that it will be noted in an ephemeral file so that follow-up is possible or if further disciplinary action may be needed.

Even if the employee has not specified that the information shared with you was confidential, discussing employee business with other employees, including supervisory- and management-level staff under any circumstances is a failure on your part to perform your expected management role.

Inappropriate or rude interaction with a customer, coworker, or supervisor is unacceptable. These include a raised voice, sarcastic comments, criticism, bullying, or impatience, as well as any demonstration of insubordination such as talking back or failing to adhere to service standards and commonly acceptable communication practices.

You discipline to help,
to improve, to correct,
to prevent, not to punish,
humiliate, or retaliate.

—JOHN WOODEN

Plan to Understand Why We Must Discipline

WHERE DO YOU hate to go? Most people (with apologies in advance to the virtuous exceptions) hate to go to their state license bureaus. Why? Because of the way the place makes you *feel*. Although it could be said that the lines are long, the staff is cranky, the rules are illogical, or even that the bathrooms are dirty, what matters is what you feel when you walk in the front door. Here's the upshot. The culture—or personality—of your organization shows. So, reason number one for doing whatever it takes to solve internal team problems is necessary because we owe it to our communities to not just look like happy places but to actually be happy places to work and to visit.

Think about the last time the person ringing up your purchases at the cash register was grumbling simultaneously to a nearby coworker about his boss, or the schedule, or the equipment, or anything else negative about his working conditions. Could you just not wait to visit there again? Could you not wait to get out of there? Probably so. Now, think of the last time truly cheerful and enthusiastic staff members interacted with you and among themselves in a positive, upbeat way, obviously pleased with their work environment and treatment. Going back there? I bet you are—I know I am.

What is important to recognize about these realities is that they tie directly back to the mission of an organization. If our mission is to serve our communities well (and that's what most of us claim), we cannot accomplish that with a troubled, frustrated, or cynical staff. Consider some of the words you'll find in standard library mission statements, because these communicate promises. *We'll be the community's gathering place. We'll be the center of the community. We'll be a safe and friendly place.* To accomplish any of these goals, we must produce and manage teams that truly exude those very concepts—and achieving that is always going to include solving problems.

Customer-service training at Disneyland is often held up as an example to follow. Why? Because *people want to go there*. It's not just the mouse, either. It's the positive, empowered team spirit given off by each and every cast member (as they're called), but also the sense that guests get when they realize they're not the only ones who truly want to be there!

From the Suggestion Box

Think back to everywhere you've worked (or perhaps to workplaces you've just heard about). Imagine you were the director reading all these suggestions slips. You've going to need to take some action (good or bad!). On each slip, fill in four real complaints you heard and, on the other four, examples of real compliments you heard. Under each, write what can and should be done about them. Why does anything have to happen? Because it's critical to recognize how an unhealthy workplace culture can affect our customers and how a healthy one needs to be actively supported. That's why we must discipline.

You really need to improve . . .	I love visiting this library, because . . .
_____	_____
_____	_____
_____	_____

You really need to improve . . .	I love visiting this library, because . . .
_____	_____
_____	_____
_____	_____

You really need to improve . . .	I love visiting this library, because . . .
_____	_____
_____	_____
_____	_____

You really need to improve . . .	I love visiting this library, because . . .
_____	_____
_____	_____
_____	_____

A HEALTHY TEAM IS A HEALTHY LIBRARY

If serving our community well is the biggest reason we must keep a team in line, the second biggest reason would be the team itself. If you're not overwhelmed when handed the job of overseeing human beings, then you're in the wrong job. Because it is a big deal. Bosses, supervisors, managers, or whatever you might call them have the *privilege* of impacting the lives of the people they manage. Impacting their lives! Surely that's a responsibility worth doing well.

There was a small branch library in a suburban community somewhere in the United States where no one on the team got along. Rudeness, gossip, challenges, and even sabotage were as commonplace as lunch and afternoon breaks. Worse, the manager didn't lift a finger to change things.

Why? Why in the world would this kind of behavior be allowed? Again, even the best-intentioned leaders will do as Jared Sandberg describes: "you just kick the can a little farther down the road—'let's have a meeting on this next month'—anything you can try to keep from having that confrontation. …What resulted was a dysfunctional department, with no discipline, no confidence in where they stood, lots of scheming and kvetching, backstabbing."

So, we're getting to the heart of the problem. It's the *confrontation* that many bosses fear, even if it means avoiding discipline when the need arises. I remember one student in a management course I taught assuring me she never wanted to be a manager because she didn't like confrontation. "What?" I asked her. "Do you think the rest of us do?"

The key here is to learn to discipline effectively, so that improvement, not angst, is the result. *What* you do to support improvement is often guided by your existing personnel policies. *How* you do it is going to depend on you and your skills.

YOUR PROFESSIONAL SUCCESS

Bottom line: it's your job. Look at your job description. As soon as you find yourself in a leadership position, you're likely going to start seeing some different requirements than those on the task lists you're accustomed to. If they don't already, your performance expectations should begin with *people*.

It's true that managers and administrators have plenty of other work responsibilities, including budgets, planning, facilities, community involvement, and maybe even customer service. But *leadership*, at its core, refers to your new responsibility—and privilege—to lead people. If you read any literature on being a great boss, you're going to find one pearl of wisdom repeated over and over. In the words of Monique Valour, "If your job involves leading others, the implications are clear: the most important thing you can do each day is to help your team members experience progress at meaningful work." Nothing can get more directly in the way of that progress than an unhealthy, unprofessional, problem-filled work environment. Therefore, like it or not, discipline is a part of your job.

When working with libraries to resolve longstanding internal culture issues that are thwarting the library's overall success, quite often I'll begin by asking how exactly supervisors are evaluated. What I often hear is that their evaluations are based on routine tasks like attendance, punctuality, even the number of compliments or complaints they generated. These, of course, are the easiest to measure. But my suggestion is always the same—evaluate leaders on their

The Long and Winding HR Road

Put on your human resources (HR) hat, consult your personnel manual or maybe even grab a cup of coffee with your HR expert and then, in each box along this pathway, write a step you would take after hearing there might be workplace harassment going on at your library. Be careful to list only steps that you would be allowed to take, then describe how you would do it. After even just seven steps, you should start to see real improvement!

STEP 2

Start Solving Problem Here!

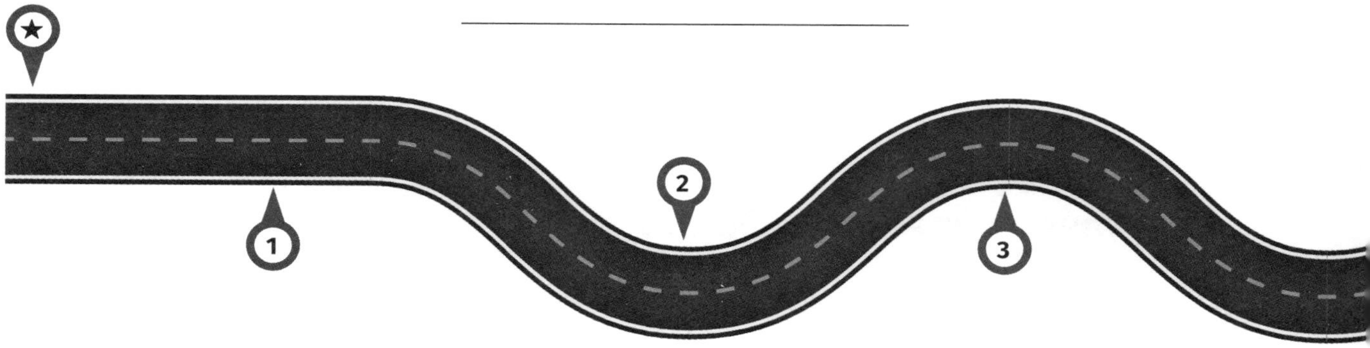

STEP 1

STEP 3

team members' success. Why? Because that's the job. To be successful, our team must be successful. We can encourage, support, and train them—all of which makes up the enjoyable part of a leader's job—but sometimes we'll also have to discipline team members in order to help solve problems. Great leaders remove roadblocks. That way, there's enough space and a pathway for everyone to succeed. So, if you're going to discipline, why not be ready to do it well?

STEP 4

_____
_____
_____
_____
_____

STEP 6

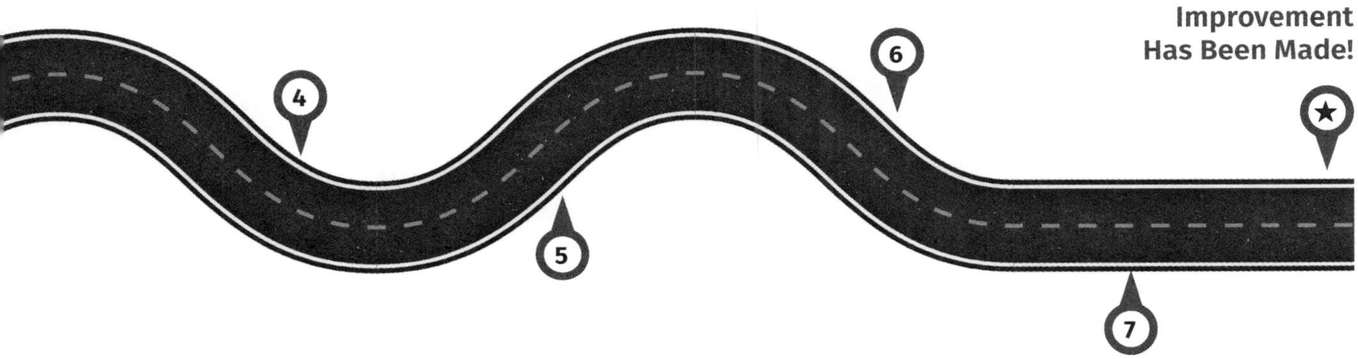

_____
_____
_____
_____
_____

Improvement Has Been Made!

STEP 5

_____
_____
_____
_____
_____

STEP 7

_____
_____
_____
_____
_____

You have to take life
as it happens,
but you should try
to make it happen the way
you want to take it.

—GERMAN PROVERB

Plan to Master the Keys to Improvement Discipline

THERE ARE TWO very important rules to effective leadership to keep in mind.

Rule 1: You can't control people.
Rule 2: You have to try.

Disciplinary challenges will come at you from all directions, and the issues they involve will be as different as the books on your shelves! In a recent discussion with graduate students, a list was compiled of the types of performance issues they might have to deal with, up to and including discipline. As expected, they listed items like tardiness, inappropriate spending, extensive absences, and so on. What often isn't mentioned by those with little experience are the more insidious, "human" issues that will inevitably emerge. Alcoholism, violence, lying, stealing, and the like almost always come as a surprise when we least expect them, and from those we would have never suspected!

The grad students were then asked to consider one of those simple but challenging issues. What would they do if team members started complaining about a coworker taking too many cigarette breaks? Because the students were too uncomfortable to consider a human confrontation to address this, almost immediately the discussion turned into a debate on the health impacts of smoking. This process took them about as far away from Improvement Discipline as they could get, because the team members would still be angry, and the coworker would still be out smoking.

So, how do you stay focused on a positive future—on real improvement? This planner will focus on four specific keys to Improvement Discipline:

1. Understanding.
2. Goals.
3. Process.
4. Moving forward.

Going back for a moment to those two key rules of leadership that introduced this chapter, we must add one more:

Rule 3: Rule 2 is not easy. But it's certainly worthwhile!

As Simon Sinek once explained, if you remain focused on improvement, you can create a circle of safety that will nurture both trust and cooperation. His best supporting example was a tech company owner who offered his team lifetime employment. Why would anyone do that? Because he knew that if his workers had the confidence that no matter what they did, he'd help them to get better and not fire them, he'd have their trust, cooperation, and continuing performance improvement.

Remove the fear. Model a positive solution. Face the problem and master Improvement Discipline.

IMPROVEMENT DISCIPLINE KEY #1—UNDERSTANDING

Something's wrong. There are complaints. You know you're going to have to bring someone into the office, try to straighten everything out, and, just maybe, exercise real discipline. Where do you start? You start by clarifying what that *something* is. What is really wrong?

- Gather facts, not fiction. View a problem for yourself, if possible. If not, get corroborating evidence from more than one person to confirm the information is true.
- As Wayne advised in the movie *Wayne's World*, live in the now. Don't try to fit today's issues into yesterday's challenges. Viewing a problem through the lens of a person's history can only prejudice your efforts to truly understand what's going on right now—and why.
- Focus on performance, not personality. It doesn't matter if the employee's a rude person. What matters is that she offered poor service to a customer, which is contrary to your customer service policy.
- Forget the technology. Meet face to face and talk nicely. Our language, both spoken and unspoken, can communicate more than the actual words we use. But if we start by picking the right words, our conversations have a better chance of remaining respectful and professional. Consider this example of language used for signage. A library had a chain across the stairway leading to the adult department that read "Do Not Enter until 9:00 a.m." After a discussion about appreciative leadership and the language that goes with it, the sign was changed to read "Looking Forward to Welcoming You Upstairs at 9:00!" Civil discourse and simple kindness can go a long way towards avoiding challenge and supporting understanding.

Say What?

How we communicate and the words we choose when we're trying to understand a problem can make all the difference. For each example, imagine you must deliver the same message but want it to sound more positive, respectful, and just plain kind. Rewrite each one.

Have this to me by
8:00 a.m. tomorrow.

_____

_____

_____

Your breaks are always
too long!

_____

_____

_____

Don't bother applying. You'll never get that job.

_____

_____

_____

Someone said you were sleeping
in the back room?

_____

_____

_____

Work it out yourself.

_____

_____

_____

Don't hire
the wrong person again!

_____

_____

_____

IMPROVEMENT DISCIPLINE KEY #2—GOALS

When meeting one morning with a brand-new, obviously terrified young reference librarian, I began by asking him to read over the personnel evaluation form he'd be getting in one year. When he'd finished, I asked him if he noted anywhere on the form where it said, "Must be able to play piano." He answered "no," so I assured him, "So, now you know I won't be asking you to play the piano or to do anything else that's not clearly part of your job."

Clarity, understanding, and confidence are important stepping stones to success and are the foundation of effective goal-setting. Let's look at how clear goals can make a difference in a library setting. If you've ever had anyone in your office for "the talk" after a rule has been broken, you've most likely heard this common response: "I didn't know that." Or even more frequently: "You never told me that." (Now, of course it's your fault a rule was broken!) Wrong or not, there's no point in arguing backwards. Real Improvement Discipline focuses on today – and on tomorrow.

- ✔ Work on fixing the existing problem by setting clear goals.
- ✔ Support, follow, and measure the success of those goals on a set schedule.
- ✔ Clarify consequences for non-compliance.
- ✔ Leave the individual with a clear understanding of accountability toward all rules going forward.

IMPROVEMENT DISCIPLINE KEY #3—PROCESS

South African author Jack Penn once said, "One of the secrets of life is to make stepping stones out of stumbling blocks." It seems logical, then, that the best process to use in Improvement Discipline is to start by identifying the stumbling blocks that created the challenge and then figure out how to best step over them. Each step will be the pieces of your process. Next, you need to get down to the details of the goals.

By when does the goal need to be met? How will both you and the employee know it has been achieved? When you will meet to talk about it next? What time? Where? In what room? Will reports or updates be required along the way? If so, how long should they be and what should they include? When are they due? What training opportunities exist that can help? What do they cost? Who will handle registration?

This level of detail reminds me of a pet peeve. I intend to address it some day in a book or article that I plan to entitle "Micromanaging is *Not* a Dirty Word." Before you get too excited, let me explain.

Let's think for a moment of your very best employee. You are responsible for making sure that person is productive and successful. That's your job, but it doesn't require much effort on your part. Certainly, no micromanaging. You pretty much just open the door in the morning and get out of her way; success

Goals to Target

Think of performance challenges you've encountered, experienced, or heard about (whether or not you were the one expected to address them). Enter them under "Challenge" in each arrow. Then, for each one, list what might have been (or were) successful, clear goals that would have led to improvement. List as many different goals as you feel might be (or were) effective.

CHALLENGE

You've called in sick 4 out of the last 5 Saturdays that you've been scheduled.

GOALS

You'll work your scheduled weekends for the next 6 months.

CHALLENGE

_____

_____

_____

_____

GOALS

_____

_____

_____

_____

CHALLENGE

_____

_____

_____

_____

GOALS

_____

_____

_____

_____

CHALLENGE

_____

_____

_____

_____

GOALS

_____

_____

_____

_____

just seems to follow her everywhere. Then, there's that *other* staff member. The one you've had to talk to repeatedly and now must discipline, because for some reason he just doesn't seem to get the message. What you need to do now—because it's also a part of your job—is what some may call micromanaging. It's really isn't, though. What you're doing is using discipline to improve the situation so that you can step back and let him succeed.

Perhaps what makes micromanaging unpopular is that it is sometimes applied to the wrong person; or to the right person at the wrong time; or to anyone but in the wrong way. Right now, you must get down to the nitty-gritty details of how, when, and why improvement will happen. Every piece of the process you lay out can be considered a stepping stone. All must be clear and be written down. You can call that "micro" or you can call that detailed follow-up. But, whatever you call it, sometimes it is the right thing to do.

Don't stop now. The balance of this key to Improvement Discipline (and the rest of your job) requires that follow up, step-by-step, to be sure that everything you've outlined actually happens and the situation does improve. Often, that's going to require one more contribution on your part.

Offer support.

Suppose the job did change suddenly, and now everyone *does* need to play the piano during programming. It wouldn't be fair to just mention that one day in a meeting or to add it into the Performance Expectations and expect miracles, would it? No, certainly not. You'd need to get a piano teacher in there—and fast!

Be absolutely certain to build into the discipline process how you will do your job as the supervisor and how you can support the improvement you expect!

- ✔ Is training needed? To build skills, you don't have to spend thousands of dollars to send someone to a conference across the county. (Although, if you can, you should send as many as possible!) There are free or inexpensive webinars that a staffer could be encouraged, or even required, to watch and respond to. Perhaps there's a workshop nearby or at your state library? Or maybe you even have an in-house expert who could be temporarily assigned to teach certain skills as part of his regular duties? One of the worst and most damaging things you can say is, "We can't afford training!" Honestly, you can't afford to go without it.
- ✔ Can you find a mentor or coach for your team member? These experts can offer support across a desk or across the country. Many professional organizations offer mentoring services, and you may find one even closer to home. Or create an ad hoc mentor relationship for every disciplinary issue. By giving struggling team members someone to talk to, someone who has been in their shoes, or someone who can help them grow the skills they need, you're giving them a leg up toward improvement and success. That is invaluable.

Getting There

Hurdles can get in the way of even the most well-meaning leaders. First, label each hurdle with something you've actually seen or experienced that got in the way of improving performance. Then, under each hurdle, list as many alternatives, solutions, and options you can think of that could have helped to get around that hurdle. Once these stumbling blocks are removed, Improvement Discipline can take place.

IMPROVEMENT DISCIPLINE KEY #4—MOVING FORWARD

Everyone loves elephants, but no one wants the boss to be one. Why? Because elephants have very long memories. Moving forward means living in the present, enjoying the improvement you and your team members have achieved together, being excited about the future, and not looking back. That means you can't hold grudges or rehash past failures or transgressions.

Discipline should always have a final result—and that means one of two things should occur.

- **Option one.** You've done a great job. You did not look away from the problem at hand, but instead you faced the challenge and conducted the discipline using all your skills to understand, correct, support, and implement improvement. Together, you and your team member have reached the improvement goals you set, and now you can move forward confidently, effectively, and proudly. As a bonus, you've also helped to solidify your own confidence that you can do the same things next time.
- **Option two.** Nothing has worked. You clearly laid out the route to success, but the team member has chosen not to follow that path. (Note the word *chosen*. I'll get back to that.) What do you do now? Give up? Say "Well, at least I tried!" Look the other way and pretend to ignore this issue? That's "No" to all. The rest of the team, your boss, the library, and even the library's customers are depending on you to discover that elusive improvement you've been seeking. And it is your job to continue trying until you have a resolution. What you need to realize is that sometimes resolution—and real improvement—can only happen after that person is gone.

Sometimes you simply must fire that person.

Terminating an employee is hard to discuss and even harder to do. But here's the thing—sometimes termination is the right option, or the only option, left for both the library and for the person involved. Ask anyone who has been let go, allowed to pursue other options, or encouraged to make a life change (whatever the semantics) how things ended up. Often, you'll hear it was the best thing that could have happened.

There's one rule of thumb to keep in mind that can help to make this ultimate action more palatable. Remember this: if you can look in the mirror and say honestly that you did absolutely everything you could to help someone improve, then you've done your best. You've given her the *choice* (there's that word again) to either get with the program and improve—with your help—or not. If the employee *chooses* the latter, then you're not firing her—she's firing herself.

You clarify the choice. The employee can decide whether to meet the improvement goal or not. She knows the consequences of both options. If she chooses the latter, then let the person go. The problem goes with her. The situation improves, and you and your team move on.

No man goes
before
his time.
Unless the boss
leaves early.

—GROUCHO MARX

Plan To Solve *What If* Scenarios

THOSE SAME MANAGEMENT class students mentioned before were later asked what they would do if one of their team members was routinely getting complaints from customers about her service. Not too tough a question, right? They came up with all the usual answers you'd expect: explain the library's mission, review the job description, provide more training, and so on. Then a few *yeah buts* and *what ifs* were added, and suddenly finding a solution got harder. That's often what happens when an issue reaches the point where it needs discipline—lots of pieces have piled up.

What if you did all of that—but none of that worked? For example, *what if* this team member, who was very skilled and experienced and did her job well, was just plain rude? And she refused to believe she was doing anything wrong and refused to change? She was also threatening to file a grievance claiming harassment. And she was getting kind of angry and obnoxious about the criticism and was even starting to yell—at you! Discipline is never easy and often it's the *what ifs* that can stump you. That is, unless you're confident using the process for improvement, and you stick to it!

Whether easy or difficult, the Improvement Discipline process can apply to any situation and, in fact, it can apply to all of them—without granting any favors, or tweaking, or manipulation for certain people. In discipline, as in most elements of leadership, consistency is your friend and applying it evenly is the very best way to build trust.

It's time for some practice. In the following five examples, you'll be given background information on an issue and the problem involved. Imagine you're the leader and you have no choice but to resolve the issue—one way or another. Your director has basically said, "Fix it!" In each case, fix it by applying the four steps of Improvement Discipline.

Consider all the facts you're being given about each situation, then fill in how you would go about following each step. Be specific and make these activities as relevant to your current situation and library as is possible for *practice* to be! Don't use real names, but do use, for example, real dates and places to talk about setting meetings. Look up, find, and name real training opportunities available to your library that you might assign. Research and refer to policies and practices already in place at your library. In other words, pretend these situations are happening right now in your organization, and follow the Improvement Discipline steps to resolve them.

SCENARIO #1—YOU'RE LATE!

Usually three people are scheduled to work the 9:00 a.m. to 5:30 p.m. shift every day, which means they must be at the desks, with all equipment up and running, and ready to greet and serve your customers when the doors open at 9:00 a.m.

This takes some work. There are sixteen computers on the floor that all need to be turned on, booted up, and in some cases tweaked a bit to ensure they're operational. There are also copiers, fax machines, and charging stations to get up and running. Even when there are three people scheduled, they're all going to be busy setting up.

What if one staff member likes to walk into the building at 8:55 a.m., amble over to the staff room to hang up his coat, chat with everyone he passes and arrive at the reference desk at exactly 9:00? He gives no thought to the fact that he's leaving his coworkers to struggle through set-up without him. And his coworkers are not happy about it.

At least five different people have complained that the coworker is always late and pointed out that this has been going on for years. The boss, who is new

---

YOU'RE LATE!   *Steps to Improvement Discipline*

STEP 1 Clarity

STEP 2 Goals

STEP 3 Process

STEP 4 Moving Forward

to the position, knows she needs to act. She stops the employee one morning on the floor and says, "You have to stop being late. You have to be here early enough to get everything going!" He smiles and says, "I'm always here by 9:00, just like the schedule says." And he walks away. Probably not the best approach the boss could have taken, right? She decides to apply Improvement Discipline steps to this situation. Back in her office, as the boss prepares to deal with this issue, she starts by reviewing the employee's personnel file. *What if* she finds that no mention of this problem has been noted before? And *what if* she is the one who has written the employee's past few reviews and has been ignoring the problem all this time? And finally, what if, when she checks the schedule she notices he may have been late on most of those days because he'd been coming from a union meeting?

SCENARIO #2—THAT'S WHAT YOU'RE WEARING?

As soon as he noticed the new librarian walk by his door in the morning, the manager cringed. "Oh no," he thought to himself. "She's not really wearing that today, is she?" Hoping against hope that she wasn't on the schedule but was just stopping by to visit, he decided to saunter casually into the nearby staff room. He nearly dropped his cup of coffee when he saw her come out.

It was even worse up close. The shirt was so tight you could clearly see what she was wearing underneath— and the skirt!? Was that the whole skirt!? Oh, man. The director was going to have the manager's head again! What's worse, he knew some of the other long-time team members had already spoken to her informally about the library's acceptable—albeit unwritten—dress code, and she'd laughed and said she preferred her own style.

Someone once said that to be certain to deal with staff legally and morally, it's helpful to assume that the person's parents and spouse are all attorneys. While this isn't meant to stop attempts at discipline, this concept can help assure you're doing everything in an appropriate and respectful manner. With that caveat in mind, *what if,* when reviewing her file, the manager also noticed that she'd recently filed a grievance claiming that the administration was creating a hostile work environment? And finally, *what if,* as she walked past his door again on the way to the public desk, the manager saw that the back of her shirt had a graphic, political message on it?

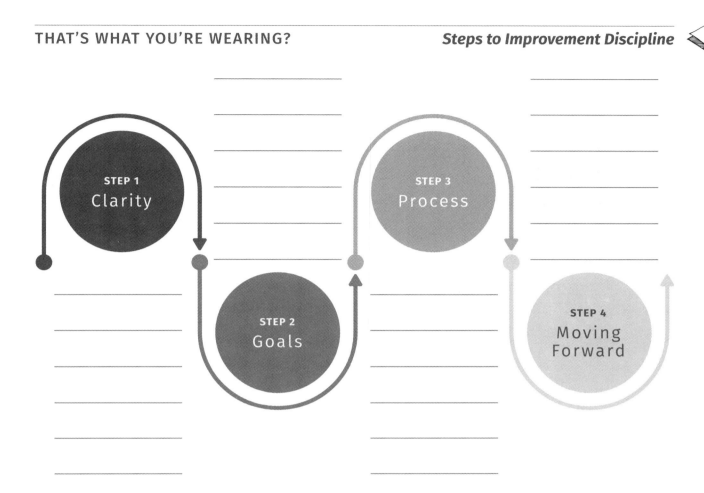

SCENARIO #3—I HAVE TO TAKE THIS!

She was a brand-new branch manager and it didn't take a genius to figure out something was terribly wrong. It was more than a little unnerving when all nine members of the children's services team walked into the manager's office, closed the door, and asked, "Do you have a minute?"

It turns out that these employees had had it. The tenth member of the team (the one who wasn't there), was driving them crazy with his personal phone calls. It had been bad enough, they explained, when it began years ago, and the employee took all his calls on the desk phone. But now, with his cell phone always in hand, he was constantly stepping away after telling his coworkers that he "had to take this call!" After asking a few more questions, the manager soon learned there was more to this issue than just taking too many breaks.

What if the manager learned that the staff member never moved far away and that all his private conversations could be easily overheard on the floor? And *what if* those same conversations often involved fights with his wife and

Steps to Improvement Discipline   I HAVE TO TAKE THIS!

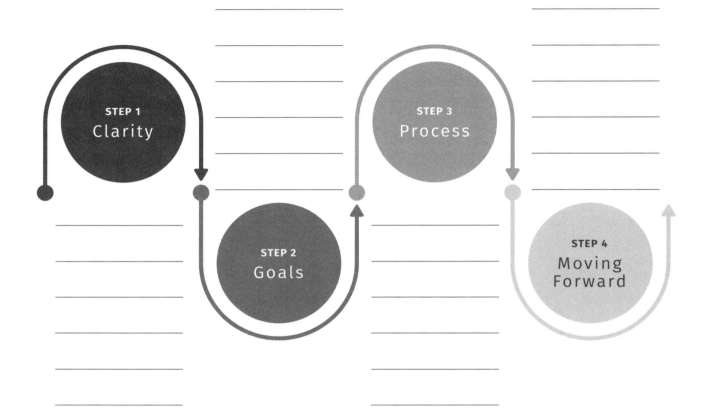

lots of inappropriate yelling, language, and even profanity? And finally, *what if* one of the people who called him most frequently was his mother, who was also president of City Council?

SCENARIO #4—ONLINE ISSUES

It drove the director crazy, but she was trying to stay calm and remember that there are generational differences she needed to keep in mind. She was holding her monthly administrative team meeting, and that one manager, the young one, was on his laptop again!

He never looked up, didn't make eye contact with the director—or anyone else in the room, for that matter. He was always typing or clicking away, and this was starting to really, really bug her. She'd asked him about it. The first time, okay, she shouldn't have asked "What are you doing on that computer?"

Steps to Improvement Discipline

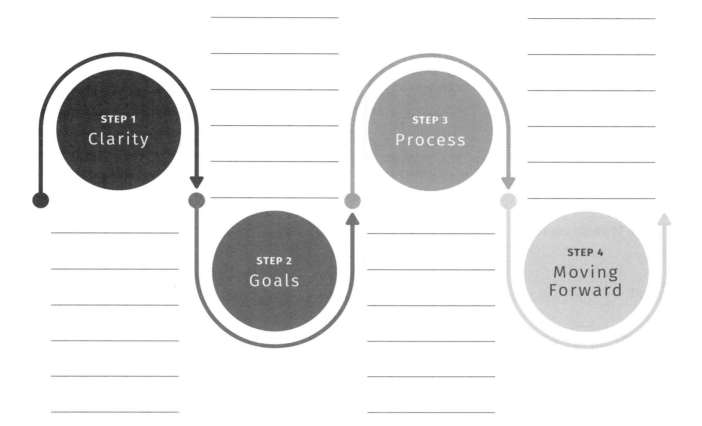

in the meeting, in front of everyone. The director had to agree it came out sounding a lot more accusatory than she'd planned. She'd followed up and privately asked the young manager to pay more attention and to be "present" at meetings—to contribute more. But he'd had an answer for everything. People his age multitasked, he said. He was paying attention. In fact, he was taking notes. He said that he was looking up research to support the programs the director was suggesting.

Finally, the director knew she must check on the manager. The policy said it was permissible because he was using a library computer and the library network. *What if* she discovered that he'd been on Facebook most of the time? And *what if* she also found out that he was in a chat room during one meeting, having a salacious conversation with a potential date? And finally, *what if* the director noticed that the manager had entered a library chat room, shared information about a coworker, and bashed that coworker and questioned the director's leadership?

SCENARIO #5—FILL IN THE BLANK

You've undoubtedly been involved in or heard about a challenging disciplinary situation much like these examples. Now that you have a good idea of how to discipline for improvement and not just punishment, pick something real that occurred in the past or is currently going on. Describe that situation on the lines below. (Remember, no real names, please, in case this planner falls into the wrong hands. We don't want *you* to become the center of the next disciplinary challenge!) After you've outlined the issue, use the Improvement Discipline format to lay out how it *could/should/might* have been handled so that real, significant improvement might have resulted.

Steps to Improvement Discipline

Fill in the blank

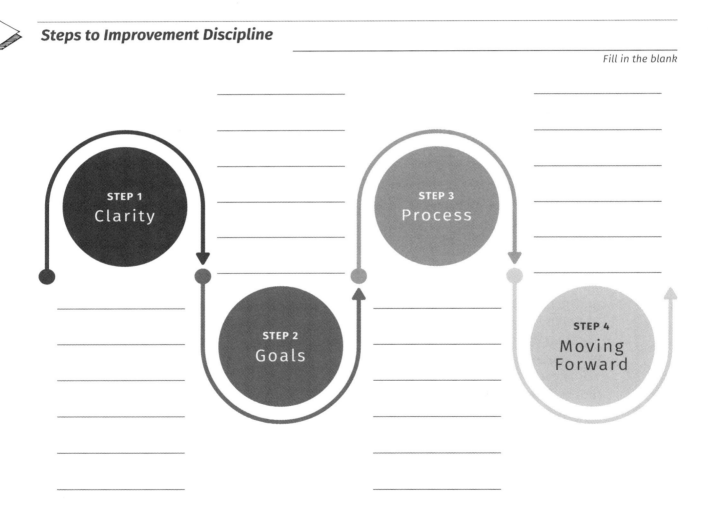

Peace is not
the absence of conflict.
It is the ability
to handle conflict by
peaceful means.

—RONALD REAGAN

Plan to Discipline Well

IF YOU CHECK almost any personnel manual or staff handbook under "Discipline," what do you see? I'll bet, most often, what you'd find is a progressive discipline chart that outlines what level of punishment is levied based on the frequency and severity of the infraction.

Be honest, have you ever found a guideline for improvement in or near that chart? Not likely.

And yet, those of us in leadership positions are often heard telling staff that they are our most important resource! If this is true (and it is), why do we treat them as though they're easily replaced?

Wouldn't it be great if we could insert an addendum, or better yet, a prologue to that infamous disciplinary chart that explains which infractions we will try to improve? Liz Ryan has some suggestions to get that list started:

Here are five good reasons, she suggests, *not* to fire employees, even if their behavior ticks you off:

1. They challenge their managers.
2. They go outside the chain of command or around the standard procedures to do or say things that they feel require the urgent attention of company leaders.
3. They don't accept the status quo, but rather question it.
4. They frustrate their leaders by playing the role of devil's advocate. They don't give up on their points of view when a manager says, "I've made my decision."
5. They make honest mistakes.

You can probably think of many more. Sure, if health or safety or legality is in question, there's not much room for improvement. But the rest of the time, any situation can be improved if you believe every person is worth the effort. Because they are.

One Step at a Time

What are you going to do now with what you've learned in this planner? What steps are you going to take to put your plan into action? As you fill out this activity, be realistic but challenge yourself to start taking steps now to incorporate dynamic Improvement Discipline into your organization. What will you do *right away*? What will you do *very soon*? And finally, what will you do *when the time is right?*

3

**When
the Time
Is Right**

2

Very Soon

1

Right Away

Sources

Ryan, Liz. 2018. "Five Reasons to Fire an Employee—And Five Reasons Not To." Forbes, January 12. https://www.forbes.com/sites/lizryan/2018/01/10/five-reasons-to-fire-someone-and-five-reasons-not-to/#64f010bf4238.

Sandberg, Jared. 2008. "Avoiding Conflicts, The Too-Nice Boss Makes Matters Worse." *The Wall Street Journal*, February 26. https://www.wsj.com/articles/SB120398045234391931.

Sinek, Simon. 2014. "Why Good Leaders Make You Feel Safe." TED Talk, May 19. https://www.youtube.com/watch?v=lmyZMtPVodo.

Valcour, Monique. 2015. "You Can't Be a Great Manager If You're Not a Good Coach." *Harvard Business Review*, February 27. https://hbr.org/2014/07/you-can't-be-a-great-manager-if-you're-not-a-good-coach.

Wayne's World. 1992. Directed by Penelope Spheeris. Los Angeles: Paramount Studios.

Zig Ziglar. 2017. Quoted in "Fear Has Two Meanings—Which Will You Choose." *Bob Garner Online*, May 2. https://www.bobgarneronline.com/blog/personal-development/fear-has-two-meanings-which-will-you-choose/.

Notes

Notes